I0428516

DEC. 07

Helping Inmates Obtain Federal Disability Benefits

This publication is based on "Helping Inmates Obtain Federal Disability Benefits: Serious Medical and Mental Illness, Incarceration, and Federal Disability Entitlement Programs," final report to the National Institute of Justice, NCJ 211989, available online at www.ncjrs.org/pdffiles1/nij/grants/211989.pdf.

Findings and conclusions of the research reported here are those of the author and do not necessarily reflect the official position or policies of the U.S. Department of Justice.

This research was supported by the National Institute of Justice and the Centers for Disease Control and Prevention under contract number 99–C–008 2002TO097 000.

NCJ 216297

ABOUT THIS REPORT

This report looks at three programs that assist inmates in preparing and filing pre-release applications for Federal disability benefits so they can continue to receive treatment without interruption after they are released from prison or jail.

What did the researcher find?

The results of the research in three study sites—the State of Texas, the city of Philadelphia, and the State of New York—indicate that helping offenders obtain Federal benefits not only can increase releasees' access to care, but also can reduce the financial burden on State and local governments that fund indigent health care systems. The most important lessons learned were—

- Interagency partnerships are an essential ingredient in the benefits application process.

- Dedicating staff to benefits tasks can build expertise and streamline administrative processes.

- Finding ways to finance treatment and monitor releasees until benefits commence is essential.

- Tracking outcomes of the process is beneficial to improving procedures and sustaining funding.

- Centralizing operations can help reduce delays and improve communication among partner organizations.

- Assisting mentally ill inmates and releasees can pose special challenges.

What were the study's limitations?

The innovative programs studied generally have not conducted adequate outcome research. Systematic data collection would aid research and help guide practice.

Who should read this report?

Correctional administrators, probation and parole officers, prison counselors, health care advocates, correctional medical staff, and health care and social workers in correctional settings.

Catherine H. Conly

Helping Inmates Obtain Federal Disability Benefits

About the Author

Catherine H. Conly prepared the final report as an independent consultant to Abt Associates Inc., Cambridge, Massachusetts, under contract number 99–C–008 2002TO097 000 with the National Institute of Justice.

On any given day, tens of thousands of inmates with serious medical or mental health conditions are housed in Federal, State, and local correctional facilities around the Nation.[1] Prevalence rates for certain mental illnesses such as schizophrenia and bipolar disorder; chronic diseases such as asthma; and infectious diseases such as tuberculosis, hepatitis C, and human immunodeficiency virus/acquired immunodeficiency syndrome (HIV/AIDS) are estimated to be significantly higher among prison and jail inmates than among the population at large.[2] In addition, for a major portion of these inmates, regular use of drugs or alcohol has contributed to or exacerbated their health or mental health conditions. Both before and after incarceration, many experience precarious lifestyles marked by periods of homelessness, joblessness, incarceration, hospitalization, family instability, and limited or sporadic health and mental health care.[3]

Although access to effective screening and treatment during incarceration appears to vary considerably according to jurisdiction, correctional setting, or type of illness, many severely ill inmates receive assessment and care for the first time in their lives while incarcerated, and many of them are released while still receiving treatment.[4] Continuing this care after release or ensuring that proper treatment commences immediately following community reentry can—

■ Increase the probability of positive health outcomes and prevent relapse.

■ Prevent the spread of disease.

■ Prevent the development of drug-resistant strains of viruses.

■ Reduce the likelihood of recidivism related to illness.

■ Insure the health, safety, and stability of families and communities that must assist and cope with releasees who are ill.

- Minimize costs to community health care systems or to prison and jail health care systems should releasees return to correctional facilities.

Helping ill releasees find ways to pay for medical and mental health care and for living expenses is thought to be a crucial part of accomplishing these goals. Options for some releasees include disability benefits available through five Federal entitlement programs.[5] The five programs are—

- Supplemental Security Income (SSI).

- Social Security Disability Insurance (SSDI).

- Medicaid.

- Medicare.

- Veterans compensation or pension funds.

Making these types of benefits available to qualifying releasees as soon after their release as possible may be a key factor in their successful return to the community. Without resources to cover care and a place to live, releasees can be at increased risk for lapses in treatment, rehospitalization, or return to

the criminal justice system. Although research to determine whether having benefits improves the health and criminal justice outcomes of severely ill releasees is only now underway or being planned,[6] researchers hypothesize that releasees who obtain benefits are more likely to seek and continue care than releasees who do not.[7]

Estimates of the number of severely ill inmates who may be eligible for entitlement benefits at release are not readily available, but experience suggests that these inmates may include—

- Those who were receiving benefits when they entered jail or prison and had their benefits reduced, suspended, or terminated following admission.

- Those who have never applied for benefits but whose circumstances suggest that they may qualify for disability benefits.

- Those who applied some time prior to incarceration but had their claims denied or closed for lack of information.

- Those who entered jail or prison with applications for benefits pending.

- Those who have received benefits at some time in their lives but lost them.

Individuals in each group face unique issues with respect to obtaining benefits, but across these groups the probability that qualifying individuals will receive benefits shortly after release may increase dramatically when benefits planning occurs during the incarceration period and the necessary paperwork is filed before the inmate is released.

Discharge planners in correctional facilities may help in cases where inmates have impaired health, limited self-advocacy skills, inability to collect information due to incarceration, and difficulty understanding the complexities of the benefits application process. These individuals are likely to require assistance from discharge planners to guarantee that applications are filed and reviewed in a timely fashion.

Depending on individual circumstances, this assistance may involve simple tasks such as helping inmates assemble identification materials (e.g., Social Security cards) and release papers and helping them contact benefits personnel. The assistance may also include more complicated tasks such as preparing and filing prerelease applications for benefits on inmates' behalf, assembling their financial and health records, monitoring the status of applications, assisting with appeals when necessary, and ensuring that releasees actually obtain benefits that are approved.

Discharge planning for severely ill inmates is still more the exception than the rule, but political leaders, corrections departments, social services agencies, community-based organizations, and researchers are turning their attention to this issue. They are looking for ways to guarantee that releasees who qualify for medical and cash benefits obtain them in a timely manner.

To shed light on how some jurisdictions are approaching this challenge, the National Institute of Justice and the Centers for Disease Control and Prevention sponsored a study to investigate and report the experiences of three sites that help severely ill inmates prepare and file prerelease applications to initiate or restart Federal entitlement benefits (i.e.,

SSI, SSDI, Medicaid, Medicare, or veterans' benefits).[8] These sites were—

- **The State of Texas,** where the Texas Correctional Office on Offenders With Medical or Mental Impairments (TCOOMMI), part of the Texas Department of Criminal Justice, has a Memorandum of Understanding (MOU) with the Social Security Administration (SSA) to aid inmates with mental illness, mental retardation, or physical disabilities to file prerelease applications for SSI and SSDI.[9]

- **Philadelphia County (City of Philadelphia), Pennsylvania**, where individuals in the Coordinating Office for Drug and Alcohol Programs (CODAAP) of the City of Philadelphia Behavioral Health System have established an informal agreement with the Philadelphia County Assistance Office of the Pennsylvania Department of Public Welfare to expedite access to Federal or State medical assistance for parolees from the city jail who participate in the city's Forensic Intensive Recovery (FIR) Program.

- **The State of New York,** where the Division of Parole has established an MOU with SSA to file prerelease applications for SSI and SSDI for severely mentally and medically ill inmates housed in State prisons.

Although their inmate populations and benefits assistance procedures differ, all three sites—

- Provide benefits assistance to sentenced jail or prison inmates prior to release.

- Target inmates who have been screened (and, in many cases, treated) for medical or mental illnesses while incarcerated.

- Rely on interagency partnerships to help inmates to initiate benefits claims.

- Have several years' experience assisting inmates with benefits applications.

Programs in three sites

The experiences of the three sites show that arranging for severely ill offenders to qualify for Federal entitlements not only facilitates access to community-based care but also can reduce the financial burden on State and local governments that fund indigent health care systems and allow community-based service providers to increase the number of disabled offenders served. Nonetheless, to varying degrees the sites have learned that helping offenders obtain benefits can be a challenging enterprise. (See "Challenges in the Benefits Application Process.")

The Texas Correctional Office on Offenders With Medical or Mental Impairments. TCOOMMI, which offers institutional and community-based services to juvenile and adult offenders with special needs (including those with mental illness, mental retardation, or terminal illness), was created by the State legislature in 1987. After a decade of administering TCOOMMI programs, staff saw the need to develop a consistent and effective process to aid these offenders in applying for Social Security, medical, and other benefits. Experience demonstrated considerable variation in the processing of parolees' and probationers' SSI and SSDI applications. In addition, although the Social Security Administration allows residents of public institutions to submit prerelease applications

CHALLENGES IN THE BENEFITS APPLICATION PROCESS

Program participants in the three sites identified a number of challenges in the benefits applications process:

■ **Staff resistance.** Some staff and professionals may resist assisting inmates because they feel that offenders do not deserve this type of assistance. Corrections staff, including contract medical and mental health staff, may not view benefits planning as part of their job descriptions and may resist participating in the process because it places additional burdens on their time. Parole officers may not assign high priority to having parolees apply for or obtain benefits.

■ **Applicant impairments.** Illiteracy, language barriers, and physical and mental health conditions can make it difficult for severely ill offenders to participate effectively in the application process. Illness may also impair their memory of prior treatment.

■ **Offender resistance.** Inmates may refuse to participate in making prerelease applications for SSI or SSDI only to discover after release that they cannot support themselves or obtain care. Parolees who have obtained prerelease approval for benefits may not follow through with obtaining benefits following release.

■ **Disability determination delays.** Even when applications for SSI or SSDI are filed prior to release, review of those applications can take a long time. As a result, benefits may not start for weeks or months after release.

■ **High rates of denial for SSI.** Initial SSI applications are often denied, which necessitates appeals that produce significant delays. If releasees do not have help filing appeals following release or cannot be located, they may lose the opportunity to obtain benefits.

■ **Lack of information.** Medical and mental health records necessary to substantiate the nature and duration of disability may be difficult to obtain because offenders typically have seen multiple health care providers in the community. In addition, correctional records may be inaccurate or incomplete.

■ **Inability to locate releasees.** Even if they receive medical approval prior to release, releasees who cannot be located are likely to have their SSI or SSDI applications closed for lack of important information.

for benefits, application submissions prior to release were typically limited to the few inmates whose work histories allowed them to apply for SSDI or whose illnesses were terminal. Most TCOOMMI participants were instructed to wait until after release to file their benefits applications, which generally resulted in a 3- to 4-month delay before they heard whether the applications were approved. Releasees with severe mental illness were especially vulnerable during this period, often failing to stabilize in the community when they lacked an income and medical assistance.

Federal benefits were critical to help offset the huge drain that releasees placed on State and county indigent resources, which were stretched to their limits. Further, staff realized that additional clients could be served if Federal benefits were available to cover some or all of the cost of services paid by TCOOMMI. Believing strongly that TCOOMMI clients who received medical and cash assistance shortly after release would be less likely to require emergency hospitalization or to reoffend to obtain income, staff approached the State legislature for authorization to launch a pilot program to aid inmates with benefits applications prior to release. In July 1999, the legislature authorized the Social Security Pilot Project. The Texas Department of Criminal Justice and SSA signed an MOU to process inmates' prerelease applications for SSI and SSDI. The MOU specifies that applications for Social Security benefits may be filed 90 days prior to an offender's scheduled release date and applicants may receive medical approval of their applications prior to release.

Operating the benefits pilot. The Pilot Project targets adult inmates with special needs who are eligible for one of two types of TCOOMMI services:

- **Medically Recommended Intensive Supervision (MRIS),** an early parole program for inmates who are sentenced to serve nonaggravated felonies and who are elderly, physically handicapped, mentally ill, terminally ill, or mentally retarded, or who have a condition requiring long-term care.

- **Continuity of Care (COC),** which offers formal prerelease and postrelease planning and aftercare services to inmates and releasees who have certain psychiatric diagnoses or are mentally retarded, physically handicapped, terminally ill, HIV positive, or elderly.

Twelve full- or part-time benefits eligibility specialists assist inmates eligible for MRIS or COC services with all applications for Federal entitlements (e.g., SSI, SSDI, food stamps, AIDS medications, veterans' benefits). Up to 120 days prior to an inmate's projected release date, TCOOMMI staff notify a benefits eligibility specialist that an inmate from a target unit is scheduled for release. The eligibility specialist contacts SSA to verify the inmate's Social Security number, citizenship, and current benefits status. He or she then meets with the inmate at the correctional facility, completes a prescreening questionnaire to determine if the offender will have difficulty obtaining or maintaining employment, receives permission from the inmate to initiate an SSI/SSDI application, and obtains signatures on release-of-information documents.

Depending on the nature of the inmate's disability, eligibility specialists work with prison mental health or medical staff to compile institutional documentation for disability applications. A specialist checks automated records from the Mental Health and Mental Retardation agency and Department of Human Services[10] to ascertain whether those agencies ever treated the applicant prior to incarceration. Whenever possible, the eligibility specialist also gathers records from any community-based providers the inmate saw prior to incarceration. The eligibility specialist then submits the application packet, including medical and mental health documentation, to SSA; monitors the review status of the application; and, if benefits are denied while the applicant is still incarcerated, assists inmates with appeals.

After filing a claim, the eligibility specialist keeps SSA informed regarding the inmate's release status, release date, and any changes in the applicant's expected postrelease address or telephone number. The eligibility specialist also maintains contact with the Disability Determination Services (DDS) examiner assigned to the case to assist with obtaining any additional information (e.g., mental status examinations, consultative examinations) SSA may require to complete its review.

Following release, an individual's file is transferred to the Mental Health and Mental Retardation agency or Department of Human Services office nearest the area where the offender will reside. In most cases, an eligibility specialist or COC caseworker at that location is assigned to monitor the SSA application, which includes providing additional information if the claim is open, assisting with appeals if the claim has been denied, or ensuring that the offender takes the necessary steps to have benefits begin (e.g., reporting to SSA so they may confirm income, resources, and residence; reporting to the Department of Human Services to start Medicaid).

Data on the filing and decision status of benefits applications (including data on inmates who refuse to submit applications) are reported to TCOOMMI staff and entered daily into a computer file. TCOOMMI staff then prepare statistical tables and distribute benefits status reports to the Mental Health and Mental Retardation agency and regional Department of Human Services staff who will provide services to clients following release. Weekly, monthly, and quarterly reports on the status of applications managed by eligibility specialists in each contracting agency are also forwarded to TCOOMMI's director, who uses the information to assess how different agencies and contractual staff handle their responsibilities for the benefits process.

Exhibit 1 illustrates the process for prerelease applications for SSI and SSDI used in the TCOOMMI programs.

Outcome of the pilot project. TCOOMMI's benefits data show that the pilot project has succeeded in helping inmates obtain Social Security benefits, but it is a challenging task. Of 1,686 individuals referred to benefits eligibility specialists in the first 9 months of fiscal year 2002, 1,076 (64 percent) did not submit applications to SSA. Most refused to apply.[11] Reportedly, some believe they are capable of working, others do not feel they are ill enough to warrant receiving benefits, and still others do not want the perceived stigma of being welfare recipients. Once released, many apply for

Exhibit 1. Processing Inmates' Prerelease Applications for SSI and SSDI in Texas

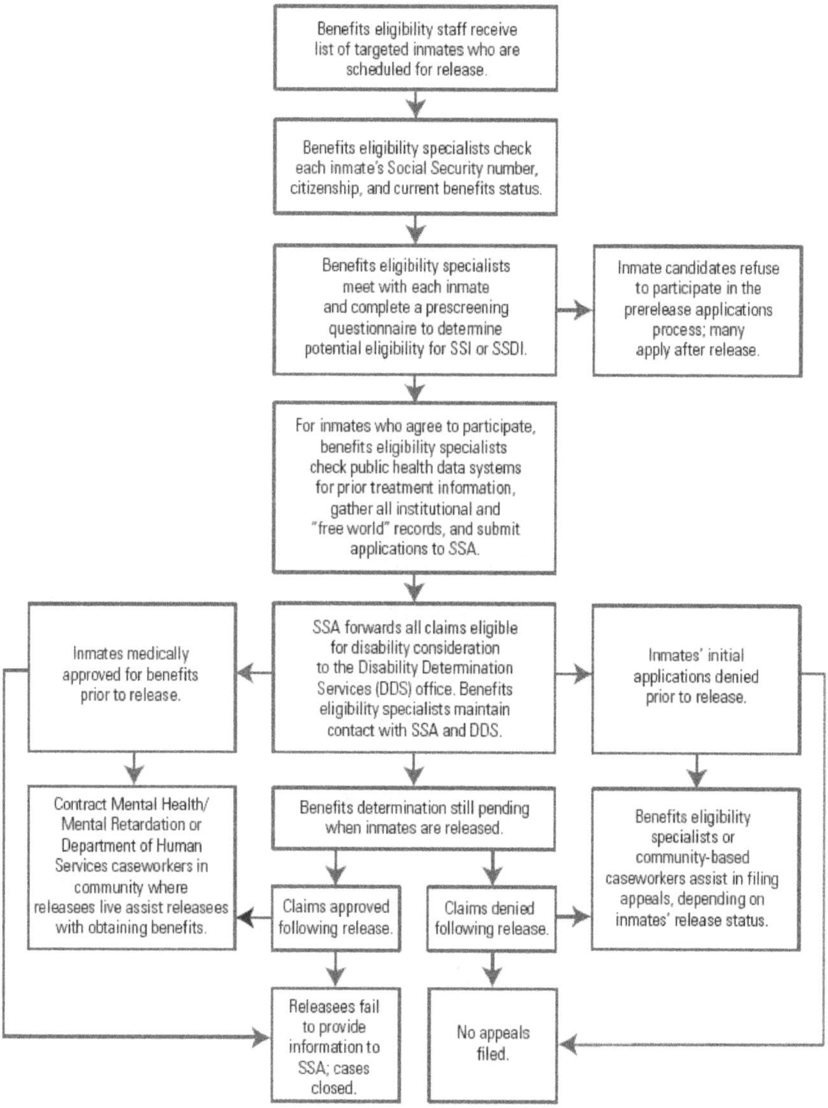

Benefits eligibility staff receive list of targeted inmates who are scheduled for release.

Benefits eligibility specialists check each inmate's Social Security number, citizenship, and current benefits status.

Benefits eligibility specialists meet with each inmate and complete a prescreening questionnaire to determine potential eligibility for SSI or SSDI.

Inmate candidates refuse to participate in the prerelease applications process; many apply after release.

For inmates who agree to participate, benefits eligibility specialists check public health data systems for prior treatment information, gather all institutional and "free world" records, and submit applications to SSA.

SSA forwards all claims eligible for disability consideration to the Disability Determination Services (DDS) office. Benefits eligibility specialists maintain contact with SSA and DDS.

Inmates medically approved for benefits prior to release.

Inmates' initial applications denied prior to release.

Contract Mental Health/ Mental Retardation or Department of Human Services caseworkers in community where releasees live assist releasees with obtaining benefits.

Benefits determination still pending when inmates are released.

Benefits eligibility specialists or community-based caseworkers assist in filing appeals, depending on inmates' release status.

Claims approved following release.

Claims denied following release.

Releasees fail to provide information to SSA; cases closed.

No appeals filed.

9

benefits because they realize that their expectations were unrealistic or their views were naive. In delaying the process, they lose precious time and money. Of the 610 cases processed by SSA in the first 9 months of fiscal year 2002, 297 (49 percent) were approved, 232 (38 percent) were denied, and 81 (13 percent) were awaiting a decision.

The application success rates vary across benefits eligibility specialists. One specialist had a 92-percent approval rating in fiscal year 2002. The keys to his success were his attention to detail, ability to obtain supporting medical examinations or documentation, and responsiveness to requests for additional information. TCOOMMI has capitalized on his acumen by having him train other benefits specialists around the State.

Anecdotal evidence suggests that by improving procedures and staffing arrangements, the benefits pilot has helped inmates and staff alike:

■ What was once a reactive process with few standards and relatively ad hoc identification of potentially eligible inmates is now a proactive one, with a system for identifying candidates, written procedures, dedicated staff, and measurable outcomes.

■ Filing applications prior to release means that more inmates now have benefits when they leave institutions than in the past.

■ Having dedicated eligibility specialists prepare benefits applications and gather medical records has reduced the burden on prison medical staff that once had sole responsibility for preparing the applications and sometimes felt overwhelmed at having benefits tasks added to their numerous treatment responsibilities.

■ Because eligibility specialists screen prospective applicants, provide considerable medical and mental health documentation with the applications, and offer prompt support if questions arise during the review process, State DDS processing of inmate applications is reportedly more efficient than in the past.

■ Finally, even when finding applicants following release is difficult, TCOOMMI's tracking procedures are usually very effective and most applicants are located.

The City of Philadelphia's Forensic Intensive Recovery Program. Since 1993, the Coordinating Office for Drug and Alcohol Abuse Programs of the City of Philadelphia's Behavioral Health System has administered the FIR Program, which provides behavioral health treatment, case management, and vocational services to individuals released via early parole or reparole from the Philadelphia Prison (local jail) System.

Inmates with substance abuse disorders who have served at least half their minimum sentences, have 6 months to a year left on their sentences, and pose no threat to the community are referred to FIR. Candidates are screened while incarcerated, and those who qualify for program services are recommended for early parole. If approved for FIR, clients are released to residential or intensive outpatient treatment programs.

Originally intended to reduce jail crowding by providing a minimum of 250 community-based treatment slots, and funded initially with city grant money totaling $3.3 million, FIR now serves 1,300 participants and has a total budget of $20 million. Federal and State medical assistance dollars,[12] which support the treatment services of 66 providers across the city, are the major sources of funding. Less than one-fifth of the budget ($3.6 million) comes from city funds and State grants, which support the salaries of a medical assistance coordinator (who helps inmates apply for benefits), clinical evaluators, case managers, vocational education staff, and supervisors.

A key reason for the increased size of the FIR Program, despite virtually static core funding and cuts in other funding sources, is that program managers have found ways to facilitate client access to medical assistance. In 1999, when they realized that medical assistance could play a significant role in defraying program costs, CODAAP staff met with staff at the Philadelphia County Assistance Office (which is operated by the Pennsylvania Department of Public Welfare [DPW] and is responsible for the administration of cash, food stamps, Medicaid, and energy assistance benefits) to discuss ways to improve the medical assistance application process for FIR participants. These efforts resulted in significant changes in the existing medical assistance applications process and increases in the number of FIR clients covered.

Streamlining medical assistance claims for FIR clients. At the inception of the FIR Program, clients were released without medical assistance. Individual, community-based treatment providers transported released FIR clients to one of 19 different county assistance offices to initiate benefits claims. This system increased the risk of client flight, interrupted treatment, and required considerable DPW staff time because multiple DPW workers were involved in making decisions and multiple visits were often necessary before eligibility was established. Moreover, it took between 30 and 45 days for clients to enroll initially in Medicaid and up to 90 days more to enroll in Community Behavioral Health, a managed care program. Until Community Behavioral Health enrollment was complete, FIR's program managers had to pay for client care with Behavioral Health Special Initiative moneys—State funds allocated for indigent residents who are not eligible for medical assistance—which severely drained available resources

and limited the number of clients the program could serve.

In 2000, through an informal agreement, CODAAP, FIR, the Defender Association of Philadelphia,[13] and the Philadelphia County Assistance Office devised a method to streamline the applications process and reduce the drain on Behavioral Health Special Initiative funds. Three concepts formed the foundation of the multifaceted reform:

■ The application process was centralized to a single assistance office.

■ Benefits applications were completed while FIR candidates were still incarcerated.

■ A medical assistance coordinator was assigned to help inmates complete applications, and one income maintenance caseworker reviewed the applications.

See exhibit 2, "Weekly Processing of FIR Clients' Medical Assistance Applications."

Outcome of FIR's modified medical assistance process. Streamlining the medical assistance application process has had positive outcomes for

Exhibit 2. Weekly Processing of FIR Clients' Medical Assistance Applications

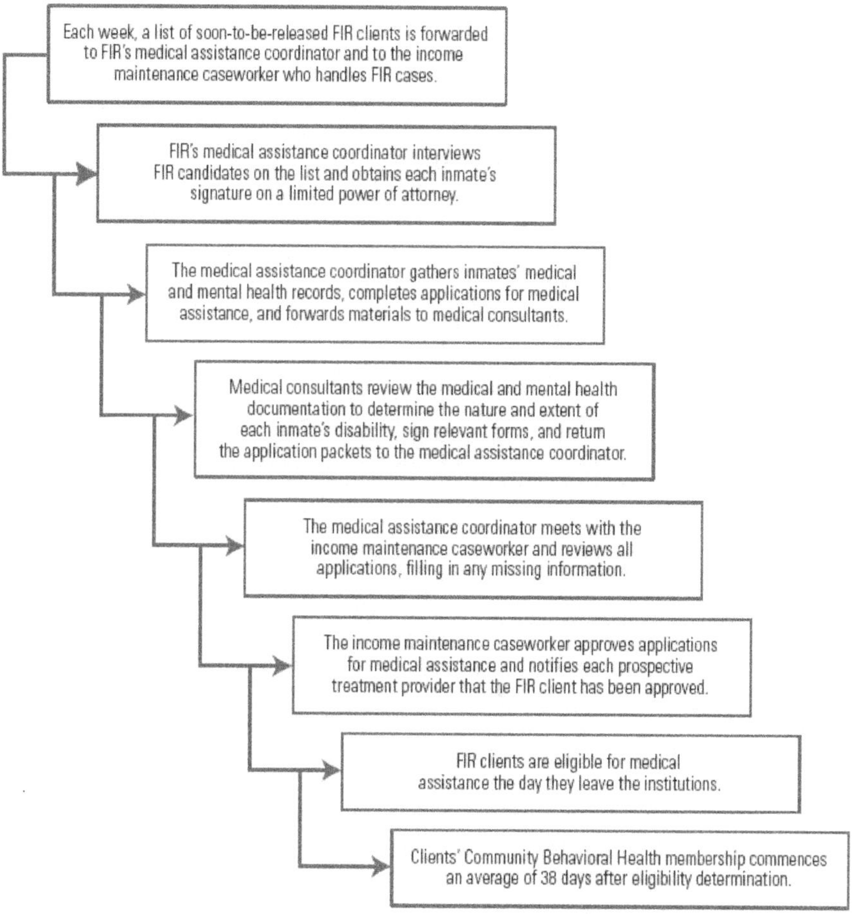

Each week, a list of soon-to-be-released FIR clients is forwarded to FIR's medical assistance coordinator and to the income maintenance caseworker who handles FIR cases.

FIR's medical assistance coordinator interviews FIR candidates on the list and obtains each inmate's signature on a limited power of attorney.

The medical assistance coordinator gathers inmates' medical and mental health records, completes applications for medical assistance, and forwards materials to medical consultants.

Medical consultants review the medical and mental health documentation to determine the nature and extent of each inmate's disability, sign relevant forms, and return the application packets to the medical assistance coordinator.

The medical assistance coordinator meets with the income maintenance caseworker and reviews all applications, filling in any missing information.

The income maintenance caseworker approves applications for medical assistance and notifies each prospective treatment provider that the FIR client has been approved.

FIR clients are eligible for medical assistance the day they leave the institutions.

Clients' Community Behavioral Health membership commences an average of 38 days after eligibility determination.

the FIR Program and for providers. It has resulted in a dramatic increase in the number of clients receiving medical assistance. Of the 2,329 applications for medical assistance acted on by DPW between July 1, 2000, and October 11, 2002, 97 percent were approved for eligibility. Between fiscal years 2000 and 2001, the percentage of FIR clients receiving medical assistance more than doubled, from 38 percent to 90 percent. In addition, shifting responsibility for benefits applications to a single benefits case manager and completing applications prior to release has significantly reduced the client flight rate and has reduced disruption in treatment associated with filing applications after release. Assigning a single DPW staff person to process FIR claims and having that person coordinate with a single medical assistance coordinator has reduced the amount of time that DPW staff must spend processing applications and has helped standardize applications review.

Benefits strategy for prison inmates in New York State. Since 1988, the New York State Division of Parole has had an MOU with SSA to support prerelease applications for SSI and SSDI benefits.

Background. The original MOU, which had few specific protocols, was updated in 2000 to include a more formalized application process and additional partners. In addition to the Division of Parole and SSA, the partnership now includes medical relations staff from the Division of Disability Determination (DDD) in the State's Office of Temporary and Disability Assistance; the State Office of Mental Health, which provides inmates with mental health care and discharge planning; and the Department of Correctional Services' Health Services, which provides medical care to inmates.

Following the signing of the updated MOU, Division of Parole, SSA, and DDD staff offered statewide training on the process, procedures, forms, and decisionmaking steps required for effective implementation. In addition, to bolster participation and become a more active partner in the discharge planning process, SSA identified contacts in each of its field offices who could respond to questions from parole, mental health, and corrections staff.

The multistage application process outlined in the

revised MOU involves identifying severely medically and mentally ill inmates eligible for SSI or SSDI benefits prior to release, completing and filing paperwork, filling in information to ensure the applications are complete, and monitoring outcomes once the completed applications have been submitted to SSA. According to the MOU, prerelease applications may be submitted to SSA up to 120 days prior to an inmate's anticipated release date. See exhibit 3, "New York's Processing of Prerelease Applications for SSI and SSDI."

Strategy outcomes. Division of Parole officials estimate that between 200 and 400 prerelease applications are submitted annually. Although data on outcomes are not maintained, anecdotal evidence from staff involved in the program suggests that a significant portion of these applications are denied. The high denial rate is not surprising given that State DDD records indicate that statewide only about 38 percent of initial claims for SSI are approved. Reasons that inmate applications are denied include the following:

■ Applicants cannot be located following release (e.g.,

because they fail to appear at their designated parole office, move from their approved residences, or are not under parole supervision). In these cases, even if applicants have been medically approved by DDD prior to release, their cases will be coded as "whereabouts unknown" by SSA and then closed for lack of information.

■ Releasees leave institutions while their applications are still under review by DDD, reportedly because release dates cannot always be anticipated accurately 120 days in advance of release. This is especially true for parole violators—one-third of new admissions to New York's prison system—who often move through the system quickly with little time for discharge planning before release. Their applications are often filed 60 days or less before release. In these cases, if DDD officials cannot find them following release to obtain additional documentation (e.g., consultative examinations), or if their field parole officer does not make benefits a priority, applications may again be closed for lack of information.

Exhibit 3. New York's Processing of Prerelease Applications for SSI and SSDI

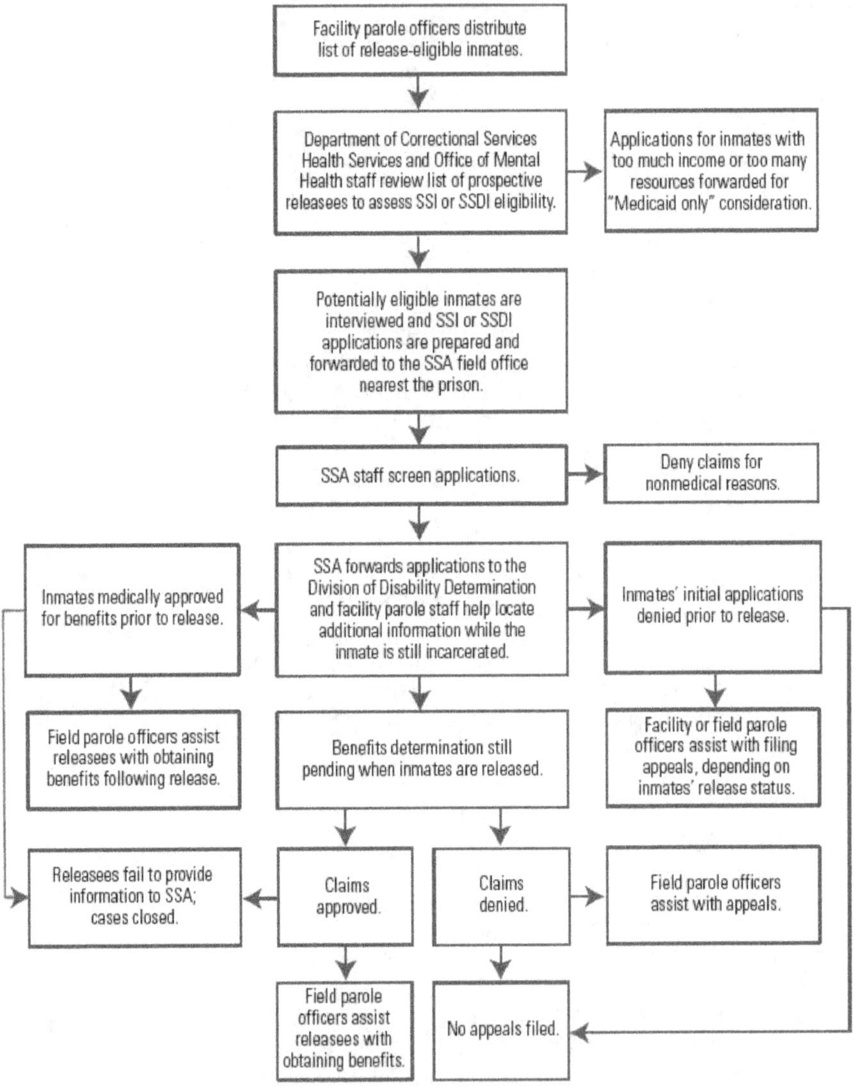

Facility parole officers distribute list of release-eligible inmates.

↓

Department of Correctional Services Health Services and Office of Mental Health staff review list of prospective releasees to assess SSI or SSDI eligibility. → Applications for inmates with too much income or too many resources forwarded for "Medicaid only" consideration.

↓

Potentially eligible inmates are interviewed and SSI or SSDI applications are prepared and forwarded to the SSA field office nearest the prison.

↓

SSA staff screen applications. → Deny claims for nonmedical reasons.

↓

Inmates medically approved for benefits prior to release. ← SSA forwards applications to the Division of Disability Determination and facility parole staff help locate additional information while the inmate is still incarcerated. → Inmates' initial applications denied prior to release.

↓   ↓   ↓

Field parole officers assist releasees with obtaining benefits following release.   Benefits determination still pending when inmates are released.   Facility or field parole officers assist with filing appeals, depending on inmates' release status.

↓   ↓   ↓

Releasees fail to provide information to SSA; cases closed. ← Claims approved.   Claims denied. → Field parole officers assist with appeals.

↓   ↓

Field parole officers assist releasees with obtaining benefits.   No appeals filed.

- Applications are denied because applicants are nonqualified aliens.

- Applications may be denied because important medical records are not complete enough to determine disability according to SSA specifications or are not obtained in a timely fashion. Inmates cannot always accurately recall their medical or mental health histories; even those who do remember may have records that are difficult to obtain because the records are in multiple locations (in the community or in the correctional system). In these instances, cases may be closed or SSA may require new applications to address missing information.

- Documentation provided by prison medical or mental health staff may not be sufficient to determine the level of impairment and the effect of the impairment on employability.

- The high rate of turnover and reassignment among parole officers can mean that individuals listed as points of contact on applications and in supporting documentation may not be available when DDD or SSA questions need answering.

- Applicants whose initial claims are denied may refuse to appeal and may apply for State-funded public assistance, which is available to some individuals who have been denied SSI.

The Division of Parole is working to address some of these issues by providing written directives to all its institutional and field agents to reinforce the importance of the prerelease application process. In addition, in 2004, DDD staff began working in conjunction with other partners on a pilot project to develop training protocols for medical and mental health staff at two prisons to ensure that mental health and medical examinations and corresponding paperwork meet the requirements for disability determination.

Lessons from the sites' experience

The experiences of the three study sites suggest six lessons regarding efforts to assist inmates with benefits applications:

- Partnerships keep the process alive.

- Dedicating staff has rewards.

- Filling gaps until benefits commence is essential.

- Tracking outcomes is beneficial.

- Centralizing operations reduces delays and improves communication.

- Assisting mentally ill offenders poses special challenges.

Partnerships keep the process alive. Whether the benefits applications process is outlined in a formal MOU, as in Texas and New York, or operates through informal agreement, as in Philadelphia, many agencies, organizations, and individuals are necessary to ensure that applications for severely ill offenders do not fall through the cracks. Multiple decisionmakers are involved in determining disability so the process works more smoothly when all parties coordinate and collaborate. This also creates the opportunity for communication about the strengths and weaknesses of the applications process. Indeed, as a result of this type of information sharing, New York launched its pilot project to have State Division of Disability Determination staff train prison mental health and medical staff on ways to improve the documentation they provide. Many claims are still open when inmates return to the community—all parties must work with offenders before and after release to make sure the applications process continues following release.

Dedicating staff has rewards. Both TCOOMMI and FIR staff have seen significant advantages to funding eligibility staff whose sole function is to help offenders access benefits. For example, since the primary burden of gathering medical and mental health documentation has shifted from corrections staff to the benefits eligibility specialists in Texas, medical staff are reportedly more willing to assist in preparing applications. In Texas, specialization means that TCOOMMI's benefits staff are able to submit application packets that contain more information (i.e., including both institutional and community-based records) than in the past, which has accelerated the review process. In Philadelphia, having dedicated staff has shifted responsibility for seeking benefits from multiple providers and numerous disability examiners to just one medical assistance coordinator and one DPW examiner. This has not only streamlined the process but also has resulted in improved security and treatment outcomes for program participants. Dedicated staff can concentrate on filling gaps in documentation without having to postpone their other institutional responsibilities. Finally, having dedicated staff increases the likelihood of strong working relationships with disability decisionmakers who can rely on a quick response to their requests for assistance.

Filling gaps until benefits commence is essential. Filing prerelease applications for benefits is not a panacea. As experiences in the three study sites demonstrate, many severely ill inmates who are approached about benefits applications leave prison or jail with little likelihood that benefits will commence soon after release. Some inmates refuse assistance prior to release; many first-time applicants leave correctional facilities before applications processing is complete; some have their

cases closed because their whereabouts are unknown; and others have their initial applications denied. Both TCOOMMI and FIR staff address the gap in benefits after release by using their own program dollars to pay for services during the period between a client's release and the start of benefits. Program funding also supports clients who are ultimately denied benefits. Any jurisdiction that seeks to prevent relapse and recidivism by ensuring that severely ill releasees receive medical and cash assistance soon after release should have similar mechanisms for funding treatment and providing other support until benefits payments commence.

Tracking outcomes is beneficial. Developing outcome data on the benefits process serves several important functions. For one thing, data can provide feedback on the success of staff efforts and identify areas where policy changes may be warranted. In Texas, TCOOMMI staff can assess which contract agencies and eligibility specialists succeed in obtaining benefits and can use the information to improve overall performance (e.g., through staff training). In contrast, in New York, where data on Social Security applications are not maintained, staff assume that their efforts are largely unsuccessful, which makes it difficult for them to sustain enthusiasm for filing applications. Benefits data can also be used as a means of demonstrating a program's ability to secure entitlement dollars that offset program costs. This type of information has been used to persuade sources of government funding in both Philadelphia and Texas to continue to support program services.

Centralizing operations reduces delays and improves communication. Sites have discovered the benefits of centralizing the processing of medical and cash assistance claims. As described earlier, partners in FIR's medical assistance application process discovered that by centralizing the processing of benefits claims they could reduce the number of individuals involved in decisionmaking and significantly reduce the amount of time until eligibility is confirmed and enrollment in the medical assistance managed care organization occurs. Faced with having cases closed because inmates cannot be located following release, staff in New York's Division of Parole have also centralized processing of postrelease requests for information by identifying individuals whom SSA and DDD staff may contact with questions regarding releasees. Staff anticipate that this will help reduce processing delays and denials by making it easier for benefits professionals to receive assistance when they need it. With a similar goal in mind, staff in TCOOMMI's Huntsville office are available to field questions and provide assistance to SSA and Disability Determination Services examiners across the State.

Assisting mentally ill offenders poses special challenges. Program participants in New York and Texas who prepare applications for prison inmates noted that assisting mentally ill inmates with benefits applications is especially challenging. Data on TCOOMMI filings show that in fiscal year 2002, 47 percent of the SSI or SSDI applications that were filed for mentally ill offenders were denied compared to 38 percent of the medical claims. Individuals in both sites suggested that disability determination staff appear more cautious about approving benefits for mentally ill inmates than they are about approving inmates with a medical illness. Program and benefits staff offered the following possible explanations:

- Fewer objective criteria exist for diagnosing mental illness than for diagnosing medical illness.

- A common perception exists that some offenders feign mental illness to obtain more favorable treatment while incarcerated.

- When applicants have co-occurring substance abuse disorders and mental illness, it is difficult to determine which is the primary diagnosis.

- Mentally ill offenders can appear stable in a correctional setting because they comply with treatment and live in a structured environment where sources of external disruption (e.g., lack of housing, drug use) are largely eliminated. As a result, it is difficult to use their behavior in prison as evidence that following release, they will not be able to engage in gainful activities.

Program staff perceive that it is easier to have applications approved when the applicant has a history of mental health treatment in the community, but they noted that, because of illness and long periods of incarceration, inmates frequently cannot remember whom they saw for treatment in the community. Often an offender's first documented treatment occurs during incarceration.

Final thoughts

Helping inmates apply for medical and cash assistance can assist severely ill inmates who are returning to the community. Such assistance, however, should be viewed as only one facet of a broader discharge plan. The application process can be complicated and take a long time to complete if it involves SSI or SSDI. There is no guarantee that claims will be approved.

Relatively few inmates or releasees apply for benefits, and when the benefits involve SSI or SSDI only a small percentage of them succeed on their first try. Even releasees who ultimately qualify for benefits are likely to find it challenging to avoid relapse or recidivism unless other supports (e.g., case management services, housing) are made available.

Although Philadelphia's FIR Program targets sentenced jail inmates, none of the strategies described in this report is designed to assist persons who are detained in local jails. Corrections facilities should develop ways to inform inmates about the benefits applications process and take steps to ensure that incarcerated inmates do not lose their benefits unnecessarily.

Notes

1. Roughly one-third of State prison inmates and one-quarter of Federal prison inmates surveyed in 1997 reported having some physical impairment or mental condition, with older inmates and women most likely to report a health problem. See Maruschak, Laura M., and Allen J. Beck, *Medical Problems of Inmates, 1997,* BJS Special Report, Washington, DC: U.S. Department of Justice, Bureau of Justice Statistics, January 2001:1, NCJ 181644, available online at www.ojp.usdoj.gov/bjs/pub/pdf/mpi97.pdf.

2. For example, prevalence rates of schizophrenia and major affective disorders among jail inmates are estimated to be two to three times higher than in the general population. See Teplin, Linda, "The Prevalence of Severe Mental Disorder Among Male Urban Jail Detainees: Comparison With the Epidemiologic Catchment Area Program," *American Journal of Public Health* 80 (6) (June 1990): 663–669.

3. According to results of inmate surveys conducted by the Bureau of Justice Statistics, mentally ill inmates were more likely than other inmates to report criminal histories involving three or more offenses; unemployment in the month prior to arrest; family histories of incarceration and alcohol or drug use; periods of homelessness during the year preceding arrest; having been under the influence of drugs or alcohol when committing their incarceration offense; past physical or sexual abuse; and alcohol dependence. See Ditton, Paula M., *Mental Health and Treatment of Inmates and Probationers,* BJS Special Report, Washington, DC: U.S. Department of Justice, Bureau of Justice Statistics, July 1999, NCJ 174463, available online at www.ojp.usdoj.gov/bjs/pub/pdf/mhtip.pdf.

4. National Commission on Correctional Health Care, *Report to Congress, Volume 1, The Health Status of Soon-To-Be-Released Inmates,* Chicago, IL: National Commission on Correctional Health Care, 2001: xvii.

5. For an overview of these entitlement programs and Federal policy regarding entitlement benefits (with a spotlight on inmate issues), see "Federal Entitlement Benefits" in the final report to NIJ, available online at www.ncjrs.org/pdffiles1/nij/grants/211989.pdf.

6. Researchers at the National GAINS Center for People With Co-Occurring Disorders in the Justice System in Delmar, New York, are studying offenders with mental illness who are released from the Pinellas County (Florida) jail to ascertain whether releasees with medical benefits fare better than releasees who do not have medical benefits.

The Texas Council on Mental Impairments plans to study whether its clients who have benefits are less likely to recidivate than clients who do not.

7. Chitwood, Dale D., Duane C. McBride, Lisa R. Metch, Mary Comerford, and Clyde B. McCoy, "A Comparison of the Need for Health Care and the Use of Health Care by Injection-Drug Users, Other Chronic Drug Users, and Nondrug Users," *American Behavioral Scientist* 41 (8) (May 1998): 1112, 1117.

8. These sites were identified through a review of existing literature on correctional health care and the need for benefits and through telephone interviews with researchers and practitioners familiar with these issues. Telephone interviewees were identified through the literature review and recommendations from other interviewees. Following site identification, each site was visited for a period of 2 to 3 days, and key decisionmakers and staff were interviewed either individually or in small groups.

9. In most States, approval for SSI disability benefits automatically qualifies an applicant for Medicaid benefits. Approval for SSDI benefits qualifies an applicant for Medicare benefits after a 2-year waiting period.

10. The agency names used in this report reflect those in use at the time this study was conducted.

11. Fifty-eight percent of inmates whose applications were not processed in fiscal year 2002 refused to apply. Among the remaining 42 percent, applications were not processed because inmates' release dates changed, they had detainers pending, they were nonqualified aliens, they were transferred out of a pilot facility, or they died.

12. Pennsylvania offers two types of medical assistance to low-income residents with disabilities. One is the Federal-State Medicaid program, which provides assistance to low-income individuals with disabilities lasting 12 months or more whose primary diagnosis is not substance abuse. The other is a solely State-funded medical assistance program for low-income individuals with temporary disabilities (i.e., those lasting less than 12 months) or with primary diagnoses of substance abuse disorder. Those with disabilities resulting from substance abuse disorders are entitled to a 9-month lifetime medical assistance benefit. Many FIR participants receive State-funded medical assistance; others receive support from the Federal-State Medicaid program. Regardless of the source of the medical assistance dollars, the process by which FIR clients obtain medical assistance (i.e., filing an application with the Department of Public Welfare) is the same.

13. The Defender Association of Philadelphia is an independent, nonprofit corporation that provides legal services for indigent criminal defendants. Although funded by the City of Philadelphia, the Defender Association is not a city or State agency.

The National Institute of Justice is the
research, development, and evaluation
agency of the U.S. Department of Justice.
NIJ's mission is to advance scientific research,
development, and evaluation to enhance the
administration of justice and public safety.

The National Institute of Justice is a component of
the Office of Justice Programs, which also includes
the Bureau of Justice Assistance; the Bureau of
Justice Statistics; the Community Capacity
Development Office; the Office for Victims of
Crime; the Office of Juvenile Justice and
Delinquency Prevention; and the Office of Sex
Offender Sentencing, Monitoring, Apprehending,
Registering, and Tracking (SMART).

www.ingramcontent.com/pod-product-compliance
Lightning Source LLC
Chambersburg PA
CBHW071349310526
45790CB00018B/1394